NIGHT-EATER

NIGHT-EATER

Patricia Young

QUATTRO BOOKS

The publication of *Night-Eater* has been generously supported by the Canada Council for the Arts and the Ontario Arts Council.

Author's photograph: Terence Young
Cover painting: *Black Forest Cake* by Marnie Faunt
Cover design: Diane Mascherin
Editor: Allan Briesmaster
Typography: Grey Wolf Typography

Published by Quattro Books Inc.
382 College Street
Toronto, Ontario, M5T 1S8
www.quattrobooks.ca

Printed in Canada

for Anja

CONTENTS

SWABBING THE DECK

This evening the swabbies are out on the deck,
swabbing its speckled gray surface:
mold, bird shit, a fine layer of grit.
They are canceling
each other out, their feet are bare.

What mysteries slip through the swabbies' minds –
                              plop –
like turtles into a pond?

The stories they tell stretch as far as the koi can see.
The continents they travel lead
through the gazebo and over the bridge.

What should we call them –
            Swabbies of Life? Swabbies of Death?

Engrossed in swabbing, they don't see
the ruby-throated hummingbird
                    drop
                              faster than sorrow.

Sometimes the swabbies lose their mantras
    among the river stones.
Sometimes they kick small fires out the back door.
They are hopeless and useless
    and want another drink.

Oh, these barefoot swabbies, they are too much
trouble and tears, too many nerve endings.

Imagine a swabbie's joy as she goes about her business
in rolled-up jeans, hair in curlers. As she pushes
broom and soapsuds across a vinyl surface. Imagine
an island draped in green, nozzle turned to *jet*.

An hour ago the deck was a sheet of dirty winter ice
but now it's a summer of cattails and millet puffs,
                    it's seven reclining chairs.

        Swabbies, swabbies!
Put down your mops and lift up your eyes.
Can you see the stars climbing into the night?
Can you see the ghost-dog padding across the horizon –
                            whoosh –
like a blue-eyed wind?

MORNING CLASS

Sunlight streaming through a bank of tall windows,
an English professor in pointy suede boots. Between her lips:
the gold-tipped filter of a black Russian cigarette.
At least that's how I remember the late

seventies, the professor roaming while she lectured,
hands always in motion, bobbed hair
swinging past her chin like a little cape.
Or she paced, head down, peeling an orange.

But on the day she arrived to discuss *Herzog*,
she just stood at the lectern and pulled
from her briefcase a dog-eared copy stuffed with post-its
and began to read excerpts, four hundred pages

of Moses un-interrupted. An hour later
when she closed the novel and looked up –
You decide. Is Saul Bellow a misogynist or not? –
she was already gone, the way we're all gone

the moment we're born, our time here
so brief, the young professor gone to the place
where the nameless millions have gone,
ashes to ashes and dust to dust, so why

do I keep seeing her tonight at the front
of a classroom in a velvet maroon skirt and silk
blouse, her long neck and blond pageboy,
a woman Saul Bellow might have looked at

in wonder, about whom he might have asked:
Who is that plotting bitch? What does she want?
To eat green salad? Drink human blood? And her smile
so wide and ready her eyes would crinkle

and disappear as though, even then, she was
squinting into the light, as though her footsteps
would always click across campus, a trail
of lipstick-smudged butts dropping in her wake.

TAMARIND TREE

There are just two people left who can speak [Ayapaneco] . . .
but they refuse to talk to each other. – The Guardian

Talk to me beneath the tamarind tree. Before it's too late,
let us bury our quarrel in Tabasco's lowlands. I am old
    and my heart stutters.
Let us talk beneath the feathery foliage and wide pinnate leaves.
Only we remember the hum and click of our grandmothers'
    tongues.

Let us bury our quarrel in Tabasco's lowlands. We are old
    and our hearts stutter.
Why do you avoid me on the street, at the market, in the
    Zocalo?
Only we remember the hum and click of our grandmothers'
    tongues.
Before our blood runs dry, speak to me of kolo-golo-nay

on the street, at the market, in the Zocalo. Why do you
    avoid me?
Rest on this bench awhile. Above us pods bulge white flesh.
Before our blood runs dry, speak to me of kolo-golo-nay
and skins that grow brittle, pulp that turns to a sticky paste.

The pods above us bulge white flesh. Rest on this bench awhile
or shake the drooping branches and watch the fruit fall.
The skins grow brittle; the pulp turns to a sticky paste.
Last week another anthropologist washed up on our linguistic
    island.

She shook the drooping branches just to watch the fruit fall.
What lies between us but three sleeping dogs and a litter
    of cracked shells?
Another anthropologist has washed up on our linguistic island.
Oh to be reborn, a flat brown bean along a tree's young shoot.

Lying between us: three sleeping dogs, a litter of cracked shells.
Brother, we speak two different versions of the same stubborn
    truth.
Oh to be reborn, a flat brown bean along a tree's young shoot,
but the rain falling on Ayapa sounds a death knell clatter.

Two different versions of the same stubborn truth? Speak
    to me, brother,
beneath the feathery foliage and wide pinnate leaves.
Listen: the rain falling on Ayapa sounds a death knell clatter.
Before it's too late, talk to me beneath the tamarind tree.

NIGHT-EATER

I was born with vague memories
of locked cupboards and jam jars

taped shut, my mother's face
guiding me back to bed. In the small hours

feasting had consequences and eyes
would not close. Sleep was not the absence

of waking and waking not a ladder
of stars. I thrashed. I binged. Five times

a night I stumbled to the kitchen,
slamming into walls. On full moons

crawled through the garden,
pulling out carrots salted with dirt.

Or tore apart the garbage,
spread coffee grounds across the driveway,

a lunatic's inkblots. What
was going on beneath my brain's soffit?

How I longed to be a masterpiece
of simplicity and clean blue lines,

a sailboat gliding above the waves.
But mornings were trash heaps: a swollen glut

of apple cores and ice-cream buckets.
If I locked the last piece of cake in a vault,

my other brain, the one that saw
everything, would fish out the key.

Self-loathing assailed me
and still I prowled, I gorged –

peanut butter, cornflakes, dried macaroni.
Once: cat food. Last weekend I woke

in front of the fridge, a frozen pie
pressed to my breasts. A stranger

was sitting on the couch, staring at me.
I was naked and holding a fork in my fist

as though I'd found it at last,
the small shovel that would dig me out.

DAUGHTER AT THIRTEEN

She sighed in the bath, at the height of summer,
crossing the road, red jeans and black boots,
       trucks whipping past.

Deep inhalations, slow exhalations.

She sighed because she sighed because she sighed,
running up the down escalator. Tilted her head,
that exquisite sculpture, and sighed
as though her heart
       were a kettle boiled dry.

Pitiful sighs at the video arcade.
Off-hand sighs in breaks in the conversation.
A sigh to bring down Mammon while looking at her watch.

       Endless her sighing.
You'd think it was some kind of joke.
You'd think one sigh could not follow another
in such a weirdly moving register.

       Monotony of sighs
click-clacking on train tracks
up the side of a mountain.

Each sigh a small part of her bigger story.
Each sigh born of her childhood landscape.

Those heaving paradoxes and insatiable gulps.
What were they made of?
       Sandstone and woe?
       Ennui and neat fans of light?

Try to describe a girl's sigh and you'll come up with
an empty knapsack, the smell of turpentine and soap.

Sometimes I thought her sighs were the reason
dead wasps dropped like stars from the ceiling.
Other times her sighs bore the weight
          of car wrecks and murders.

Each sigh opening like a shutter,
closing like fish gills. In the whole world
          not enough air to fill her lungs.

Once I looked out the window and saw her
walking the breezeway beneath the kitchen window.
I cranked up the radio but how
          could she not be
too much with me, in me,
                    breath of my breath.

Above the static and voices I heard her sigh
breezeway. I heard the *breeze* and the *way*.

THE ROOFERS

Who is stomping above me
at seven in the morning,
tearing shakes off the roof
while the neighbour rushes

around his house covering
windows with sheets of plastic?
Meanwhile his wife continues
to dream the sun, moon and stars

have disappeared. Three men
and three nail guns: unrelenting.
Thin gold bullets litter the lawn.
At the end of her life I hadn't

the heart to tell my friend
her lover was a cad. Those last
days she went to him dressed
in essential oils. Arched her back

in a cinnamon storm. Off the coast
of Zanzibar bottleneck dolphins
swim in baffled circles, trying to orient
their brains. I didn't mind the leaks

in the ceiling, the arrhythmic drip
into pots and bowls, but my husband
would lie in bed, worrying *shelter,*
shelter, shelter. How much longer –

Thor and his minions, their thunderous
footsteps? Dolphin carcasses wash
up on the white beaches of Africa,
drawing fishermen from all over

the island. I didn't know two spices
hatch from a single egg: nutmeg
and mace. And cloves, ripe at this
time of year, are sold in bags

from roadside stalls. Sex lies
at the root of life, and we'll never
revere life until we understand
sex. I'm quoting someone, I don't

remember who on this aromatic
morning, the fearless gods of asphalt
negotiating the forty-five degree
incline above my head.

THREE BRIDGE POEMS

The work of a bridge is to do nothing
but span a body of water. Foolish woman,
why are you so difficult to love
as the bridge unfolds beneath you?

*

I keep returning to the bridge,
a truss of matchsticks and raddled dolls.
A honey-coloured dog sitting sentinel
at either side. White so blinding
it stings the brain, temperatures
that plunge, then spike, and there's
the yellow house I lived in
the year the river melted too quickly
and water covered the land
and people scrambled into boats
or swam to higher shores.

*

In summer a man and woman jogged
across the bridge's hot metal flank.
In winter they walked beneath it,
on the frozen lake. After their children
were in bed they'd sit up late
in the library, a room that smelled
of tobacco, and drink whiskey
and talk. Once the woman drank so much
she had to get down on the floor
and lie on her back, but she wasn't
drunk because, *Look*, she said, *I can read
all the titles, even those on the highest shelf.*

FOOTNOTE TO GENESIS

I should have said something on the fifth day, a few
    honest words, should have spoken the moment
the man and woman set eyes on each other. It wasn't
    too late to call the amorphous void back into being.
I should have said, *Let there be neither light nor darkness,*
    neither male nor female anymore. But no, I kept giving unto
them, every herb-bearing seed and great blue whale. Dazzled
    by their beauty, I turned from the look in their eyes,
look that said they *would* have dominion over each other.
    In that instant, I heard the beasts of the earth and fowl
of the air and the monsters of the sea groan and cry out.
    Long before the waters under heaven were gathered
unto one place, I knew the whole enterprise was doomed.
    The man and woman would doom it. Had no choice
but to doom it. They were what they were. Forgive me.
    I was an imprudent god puffed up with pride in my own
handiwork, and so I looked down and said, *Behold, it is good.*

THE SHORTEST DISTANCE

Laughter's like sex, he said, there's never enough.
Let's laugh, then, she said. Let's loiter
among the *Do Not Loiter* signs. Angels don't laugh,
he said. Neither do animals. Oh? she said.
How explain the giggles that ripple through
the evolutionary tree? Pity the mirthless, he said,
for they are like trained seals, barking. What, she said,
is the opposite of laughter? A man on death's door
watching Laurel and Hardy movies every day for a year,
he said, a man who believes laughter will restore his health?
For women laughter is orgasm, she said, for men it is love.
If laughter's akin to grace shouldn't God laugh too? he said.
Listen, she said, the baby's making those gurgling sounds
again. My mother said laughter's the shortest distance
between two people, he said. I miss my father's laugh,
she said, the way it would erupt somewhere deep
in his belly, break free of his body and enter the trees.

HEARTSICK

My friend is heartsick and doesn't know why.
Sometimes she falls and can't get up again.
Sometimes she topples like a sunflower,
last pillar of a weary civilization.
Or barricades herself inside a burning building

and drinks banana wine. *Don't touch me,*
she says, *I'll disappear if you touch.*
Unlike the buoyant, the heartsick
will never lift off the ground, never gaze down
on the honeycomb cities or know

the happiness of flight. Like cheap Chinese lanterns,
they blink too often or late. *Don't be heartsick,*
we say, *don't listen to that Paroxetine music,*
don't give up the ghost. What we mean is:
the heartsick are prophets. We mean:

a sick heart is the beginning of truth.
Smoking under the deck,
she reminisces the driftwood years,
living in beach shacks, no money for tea
candles, cougar at the door. At thirty-six

her life is already too long, her cells weighed down
with a sadness she cannot name. Why
do the heartsick lean against trees while they sleep?
Why do they travel to the gates of paradise
where the mandrake thrives? Born on the salt

waters of grief, they beat through the wreckage
of worlds, searching for cures or the blood
of mulberries. Tonight my friend presses her hand
on the place where her heart is. *This,* she says,
is where it hurts. If the heartsick understand anything

it is a broken umbrella dragged through mud.
They are like deer entering the forest,
knowing they will never find their way out again,
or courteous strangers wandering an uncivil land,
their beautiful mouths singing *tra la la.*

THE FEAR

Hal's daughter and I nicknamed a hangover 'the fear' for reasons that may be ineffable to more sanguine types. – B.H.

The fear grabbed us by the throat and shook us like winter.
It illuminated the trees and killed our car batteries,
but, oh, the uncommon gentleness of its plucking,
the way it understood nothing mattered
now we'd stumbled into a forest covered in wet needles.

Avoid the fear, the sanguine advised.
Impossible. It was the kiss
            before plunging into darkness.
While others ran from the fear we rushed toward it,
gutted as rag-pickers, broken as pacifists.
It had us both ways, going in and coming out.

            The fear, the fear:
irrational, passionate, always seeking reinvention.
Let the record show: the fear gorged on fumes,
            but *we* got stoned.

Was it always so maddening in its affection?

We accused the fear of many things
            but never of pulling its punches.
We admired it more than was wise, its longevity
and mathematical accuracy: a plain-talker,
            shaggy-dog story, metaphor-scant.

It ranked this high and no higher.

The fear took what might have been,
then gave it back to us, swaddled in grape leaves,
and yet, and yet, when it strode past in the early hours
we understood it was no meditation on loss,
      it was no sacred cow.
It was our own breath tracking itself
through the wilderness. It was the fear that the fear
      would outlast us till spring.

And then, Beloved, the snow began to fall.

FIRST BEAR SIGHTING IN EIGHTY YEARS

The bear circles the cabin to the sound of light
jazz on the outdoor speakers. Lena Horne's
voice going nowhere, leaves hissing rain.

Bear who's blundered out of the forest
where for centuries one tree's died
on top of another. Unlikely bear
on the southern tip of this deer-deep island,
and yet there she is
                        on the kitchen stoop,
hunchbacked dog, stately wayfarer scratching a haunch.

She wants a salmon steak, blackberry pie, kale stew.
She wants to lie down by your fire and sleep for years.

Inside your own rank den you move from room to room,
window to window, breathless, heart in your throat.
You hallucinate bear,
                her lumbering shape and shining presence.
Stinking bear who can't see can smell you through walls.

Face pressed against glass, you try to hold onto
her shifting shape, half sun, half moon,
            equinox bear
sheathed in green air passes through your eyes,
becoming wild boar, piglet,
                            no, look again:
bear is bear, rain is rain, leaves fall
on the dimly encroaching animal turning
toward you, unwashed woman
                        going feral into winter.

WHAT DOESN'T BREAK DOWN

I was on my knees sifting out Chiquita banana stickers,
toothpaste caps, twist ties, Styrofoam chips, baby rattles,
sunglasses, cell phones, keyboards, weather stripping,
triple AAA batteries, remote controls, airplane propellers,
medical waste, chaos, gravity, a house of cards.

Back aching, I sifted. During thundershowers. Dust storms.
By the moon's light. Even my dreams fell through a wire
mesh screen. I sifted until the years blew like chaff
in the wind. Until I burned with a bright and ancient joy.
The seasons came and went, the sediment at the back

of my mind growing dark and rich, and still I sifted until
the compost in the corner garden deflated like a beached
whale, and I became earthworm, beetle-mite, centipede,
protozoa, fungi, bacteria, good clean dirt. Good clean dirt?
Protozoa, fungi, bacteria? Centipede, beetle-mite, earthworm?

A beached whale deflates in the corner garden while I
sift the dark compost. Sediment grows rich at the back
of my mind, a bright and ancient joy. The seasons come
and go. Chaff blows in the wind until, burning with years,
I fall through wire mesh. I screen dust-storms, sift moon-

light. My dreams ache. I shower. Sift cards. Waste airplane
propellers, medical chaos, gravity houses, triple AAA weather
stripping, battery controls, remote baby chips, sunglass rattles,
cell boards, key phones, banana toothpaste, sticker caps,
Styrofoam twists. Chiquita, darling, I'm on my knees, sifting.

SIXTIES SECRETARIES

Quit, your friends said, get another job,
you're too smart to be a secretary.
What they didn't know: secretaries
were smarter than brain surgeons
by a typewriter ribbon mile. Could
smoke and drive a Mustang while
scribbling hieroglyphs on crossed knees.
Not waitresses, not hatcheck girls.
More like beekeepers or feather merchants.
More like knife-throwers or soothsayers.
What your friends didn't know:
those secretaries spun like radio
dials, could see through walls, penetrate
the inner sanctums of the men
whose correspondence they banged out
faster than a jet plane on eight sheets
of carbon paper. Could anticipate desire.
Transcribe the ephemeral. Had a light
touch, wore peppermint pink lipstick.
On coffee breaks flipped through
Scientific American and *Modern Bride*.
Dumb secretaries, your friends said,
clueless, unaware those women
were savants of discretion, archetypal,
synonymous with high heels and sinewy
architecture, had read all the Russian
novels, spoke three Latinate languages.
Multiplied and divided long-winded
fractions inside their bobbly heads.
Could white-out the sky.

FAMILY REAL ESTATE

for Snade

Other than Big Mouse asleep in the breadbox,
our house was perfect. When it rained my hair shrank
into corkscrew curls and my brother, whom I adored,
folded his stories into compact squares. He refused
to leave his blue room overlooking the sea when it rained.

My hair shrank into corkscrew curls. On our jagged
point, birds and otters swooped and honked.
My brother refused to leave his blue room
until a waif, lovely but stern, moved into the garage.
On our jagged point, birds and otters swooped

and honked. We didn't know who she was
or where she'd come from, the lovely but stern waif
who moved into the garage. When I asked my father –
who is she? – he just shrugged, melancholic.
We didn't know who she was or where she'd come from

but some nights, everyone asleep, she'd open a portal.
My melancholic father just shrugged when I asked
who she was. Alone in my room, I danced with my pet
octopus. Some nights, everyone asleep, a portal
would open and men in gumboots appeared like a vision

from hell. Alone in my room I danced with my pet
octopus. Which way, the men shouted, which way
to the rat? The men in gumboots (who appeared
like a vision from hell) pointed their rifles of poison.
Canisters on their backs, they shouted, Which way?

Which way to the rat? My mother at the restaurant
was carving up animals. Canister on her back,
she pointed her poisonous knife. Later that night,
the kitchen air shivered noisily. Mother was carving
up animals at the restaurant, serving meat to her guests.

The night I cracked my bedroom door open I heard
the air in the kitchen shiver noisily. There they were –
thousands upon thousands freed from dungeons.
Cracking my bedroom door open, I saw mother's guests
eating meat while the wretched of the earth streamed

down the hallway, thousands freed from dungeons.
There he was! My brother who believed in the waif's power
but not the exterminators'. The wretched of the earth
streamed down the hallway. Some day I'd turn
our lives into an animated film about talking trees.

My brother believed in the waif's power but not
the exterminators folding compact stories
into squares. Some day I'd turn into a talking
film animated with trees. Other than Big Mouse
sleeping in the breadbox, our house was perfect.

GIRL OUT OF WATER

Seeking still life model: maid from the navel up,
fish from the navel down.   – Classified Ads

How strange to drop your robe and reveal legs.
How strange to *possess* legs.
To tap your own kneecaps
as though they were xylophone keys.
How strange to make music.
Music of ankles. Music of toes.

*

Sweetheart, the artist says, it's about me, not you,
your breasts, hair, earlobes studded with pearls.
Not to put too fine a point on it,
it's about shape, angle, light, shadow.
You taking instructions from me,
raising an arm, cocking a scaly hip.
It's about being actively
passive, muse, collaborator,
inspiration, not making up your mind,
having a mind, it's about mental
vacuity, your face a calm sea
on which I inscribe the world's suffering –
its shape, angles, light, shadows.
It's about rapport, yours and mine,
you bringing something meaty to my table.

*

How strange to be woman, not legend,
nude not naked, to be rendered
in oil, charcoal, watercolour, to capture
the human imagination, condition,
to experience muscle cramps, depression,
a sudden change in humidity, the urge
to eat pizza. How strange to hang
from the rafters in a mountaineer's harness.
To be fluid, freeze into a pose,
swim through the air. How strange
to be strange: angel wings, porpoise tail.

THE BIG SIESTA
(OR: THE END OF MODERN WARFARE)

On Tuesday night all the soldiers in the world
   fell asleep and didn't wake until three days later
when they blinked twice then fell back asleep.

And the marines and the navy seals and the snipers
   on rooftops, they all groaned, *So damned tired.*
The newest recruits, the peach-faced boys, lay

down their weapons and plunged into a slumber
   from which their sergeants could not wake them,
no matter how they barked and kicked and threw

cold water over the boys' sleeping faces. Electric
   shocks zapped a few eyes open before closing
again, heads sinking into pillows and fields

seeded with uranium pellets. And the generals
   gathered in bars and canteens all over the world
to compare medals and shining careers and also

to rage against all the lazy mother-fuckers sleeping
   under their command. If word got out, their
five star asses were gonna be toast. But after a bit

the generals grew sick of hearing themselves fret
   like old women who can't find their bus passes.
How tedious their schemes of death – what

wedding party to blow to bits, where to drop the
   latest bunker-busting, phosphorescent, daisy-
cutting bomb? The generals knocked back one last

whiskey and stumbled into parking lots and foreign
   hotels while the soldiers sank into a sleep more
profound than the arch of a bridge or a girl's

sandaled foot, boys who babbled unintelligible
   sentences as the fax machines whirred and phones
started ringing and emails shot through cyberspace

with orders to get back to it, but the sleepers slept
   on, hands slack at their sides, foreheads smooth
as water, every rank and file soldier having closed

his eyes and ears to the petulant howls of the leaders
   of the free and not so free world, yes, even the hot-shot
pilots in their high-tech jets, even the gunners inside

their explosive-resistant tanks turned off the ignitions
   and voices yammering inside their head-sets. Slumped
forward, cheeks pressed against control panels they

slept like newborns for three more days and three more
   nights and then it happened – all the soldiers on earth
rolled in unison onto their sides like a flock of starlings

changing direction mid-flight then dropping as one
   onto bare winter trees, the branches now trembling
with leaves that only moments before did not exist.

ROOMS WITHIN ROOMS

Of foyers, vestibules, ante-chambers,
    fainting-rooms, still-rooms,
box-rooms.
          Rooms
             that dissolve
into cloud patterns or change
according to the water temperature.
           Rooms
in which you have wept in alabaster bathtubs.
And doors, their swift refusals or revolving invitations.
            Nooks
      that rub up against each other.
Boudoirs that reverberate,
                alcoves that betray,
pantries sprouting mushrooms.
          Passageways
that link one to the other, him to her, birth to death.
      Rooms as metaphors:
   root cellar as id,
             attic as super-ego.
You have fallen
         asleep in libraries
that accommodated the best of everything:
      miniature donkeys, ripe figs, train stations.
You have straddled hemispheres
       with both lobes of your brain.
   The cloakrooms of childhood, those damp spaces
          in which you performed
small acts of torture
        with the precision
of lab technicians. Stark rooms
   in which each scene is painted with the same
post-war brush. Yes
         to hilltop rooms

with panoramic views, to paper rooms
in which conundrums
solve themselves.
And windows.
With or without glass.
Wooden jalousies open to equatorial breezes.
Unimposing rooms
connected by staircases
that travel backwards,
multi-levelled, vertically connected, easily
identifiable: a nursery, say –
crib, diaper bucket, stuffed toys.
Storage rooms, shelves lined with broken radios.
Nineteenth century salons, lofts and solariums.
Any corridor leading to a room
in which two people
get down on their knees,
ride the wave on their hard flat bellies.
You have sipped wine in anechoic chambers,
you have passed out drunk
in a stranger's atrium.
Darkrooms in which light
is still a transformative
idea. Sculleries. A woman bending over
a sink, scouring the last bit of enamel.
No
to rooms in which children go soft
as pears. Every plaster crack
through which you enter
and leave the world.
Every tin ceiling raining rust on your head.
Rooms that enter you
the way grief enters the body.
Rooms without
hope or a plastic globe spinning in the corner.
The mudroom
in which you once heard
a voice say, *Why did he leave me for the indolent blue hills?*

SISYPHEAN

They don't come anymore, the man and his small son, but for
two years they came every Sunday, hand in hand, down the
slippery steps to the beach wrapped around the bay. The man
wore garden gloves and carried an industrial-strength garbage
bag. His son wore gloves too. No matter the season or
weather they'd scour the beach for washed-up trash, the boy
running ahead of his father: *Look at this! And this!* The ocean's
wondrous belly spitting up more and more booze bottles,
lampshades, condoms, bits of synthetic rope. And sometimes
the man knelt to examine a hairbrush or telephone receiver
before dropping it into the bag. In those moments what did
he say to the boy? Did he explain the Sisyphean task set
before them? That plastic breaks down slowly, over
thousands of years? That mermaid tears never dissolve?
Holding a mug of tea between my hands, I'd stand at the
window and wonder: was the man saying *food chain, chemical
pollutant, death of the sea?* Or was he avoiding the eye of the one
to whom he'd so carelessly given life: *What you got there, Bub –
doll's head, BB gun, baby's bootie?*

HITCHHIKER

The plot's simple, timeless: girl masquerades as boy.
This time it's your best friend disguised as a street
urchin, one of those comely 19th century pickpockets –
ripped jacket, sooty face, hair stuffed into a cap.
This time she plans to hitchhike to her Aunt Millie's,
seventy kilometers north, and it's like watching
a movie in which the heroine keeps casting confused
but enigmatic looks at the camera. The scene
unwinds to a soundtrack of doom: *I know, I know,*
but what's a girl to do, I've gotta get around. She plants
her feet at the side of the highway, sticks out a thumb.
You can't bear to watch and you can't bear not to.
Her features betray her, the fine bones and dancer's body.
It must be August, the air smells of hot asphalt,
forests burning, and when you look again
the light's all wrong and everything's in motion –
clouds, leaves, traffic. A car screeches to a soundless
halt, silence builds to a crescendo. The driver leans
over, unlocks the passenger door. You hate
this part, the girl turning to you, waving goodbye.
Don't, you shout across the median and years,
her whole life stuttering away from her on a dotted
white line. The scene moves too fast in slow motion.
And then she. And then she. And then she gets in.

WALL OF FIRE

*. . . protecting a home against fire has been an aspect of
Australian life in the bush for a hundred and fifty years . . .*
                                    – New Yorker

No damnit we'll stay right here fight it out
someone was saying not sure that's a good idea

saying bring in the door mats hose down the decks
spray the hedge turn on the sprinklers someone

was saying I've got a bad feeling about this saying
the baby's crying wish we'd left earlier saying shut

off the gas close the windows soak everything then
get inside someone was saying she won't stop crying

saying I'm scared honey saying a really *really* bad
feeling someone was saying we're tougher than that

saying Christ the heat like a Turkish prison in here
saying too late to leave anyhow saying baby's hyper-

ventilating saying I blame you for this saying sky's
blacker than hell saying hell's not black someone

was saying please everyone calm the fuck down have
a beer it's not the end of the world saying tougher

than what tougher than who saying don't talk like
that saying I'm scared shitless saying fill the baby's

tub saying should've gone earlier saying hey she's not
crying anymore why isn't she crying someone was saying

circle the baby make a ring around the tub saying
you bastard I'll never forgive you for this saying look

at her face saying fuckfuckfuck the light holy Christ
saying here it comes our blood our future our tribe.

FIRST DATE

Red velvet hangs over the saloon window
the way it would hang over a thickly woven plot:
near-sighted boy, broken scooter. She wants
to know: What *is* a bordello, exactly? A logical man,
he's interested in the way one thing leads to another
so weaves her into a thick plot: a near-sighted boy,
a broken scooter. The night's a loopy salad,
though glimmerings of clarity pass between them.
He's a logical man, interested in the way
one thing leads to another. For instance, the way
a kiss can lead to the whole vegetable garden.
The night's a loopy salad, though glimmerings of clarity
pass between them. He just asks that artichoke
be artichoke, radish be radish, that a kiss lead to the whole
vegetable garden. She wants to bring him up close,
then, lie down in the summerhouse. He just asks
that artichoke be artichoke, radish be radish,
to drink his wine and pay the bill. She wants to bring him
up close. She wants to lie down in a summerhouse.
Out on the sidewalk he pauses to light her cigarette.
They've drunk their wine, paid the bill. Listen, she says:
the sound of water rushing over a ledge of the earth.
Out on the sidewalk he pauses to light her cigarette.
They could be any young couple on a bridge, heads bent
together. The sound of water rushes over a ledge of earth
and still he hasn't answered: what *is* a bordello,
exactly? Like any young couple standing on a bridge,
they bend their heads together. Red velvet hangs
over the saloon window the way it would hang.

ON THE ROAD TO PRITCHARD

On the road to Pritchard their marriage came apart
in bite-sized pieces, it tumbled through the air
like leaves in autumn, except it was summer,
July, and the children in the back seat
were shredding their wings. A blackbird
flew in one window and out the other,
and cows, cows, cows. *On the Road to Pritchard*

might have been a documentary of an ordinary
family driving an ordinary country road
on a day when the sweet-burn
of distant forests entered its future memories.
They were that far out, the landscape that outlandish,
and so they kept driving over cattle
guards and bridges, past goats and aluminum shacks.

They'd heard love was hard over the long haul,
but love wasn't the problem, love hovered
like a helicopter above a field before slashing to earth,
wounded by light. How does a road know
where to begin, where to end? On either side
the ground fell away or bled into sinuous grasses.
A bear blundered out of the trees and squatted

on its haunches. What did they know of Pritchard itself?
Not a town or village, not even a hamlet.
It was a general store, nothing to speak of unless
to speak of newspapers and sticks of beef jerky, a pit
stop to fill up the gas tank, buy Fudgesicles and beer.
They stretched their legs, then turned the car around,
and drove back the same way they'd come, over train

tracks and river, past acres of slow-growing ginseng,
drove for the sake of it, for the sweeping gold vistas
and tumbling tumbleweed, drove for the children,
ice-cream dribbling down their chins, drove
for the marriage that would survive the sterile
voice of the voice-over, drove to the place
where the pavement stopped and the gravel began.

GIFT FROM ITALY

for Cynthia

I'd never been so pleased to set the cutlery
and glasses in their correct places,
nor had I cared for
etiquette or beauty the way
I cared for etiquette and beauty
the night I spread that linen cloth
over the table, olives and vines
looping its border. And never
so sloppy spooning beets from serving bowl
to plate, a small drop seeping into
the fabric so that everyone ceased shaking
napkins across laps and stared
at the no longer pristine rectangle
that had transformed the basement
kitchen into a lofty room
overlooking a piazza bathed
in burnt light. You watch a stain
like that spread and think *ruined*,
you think why not head for the hills
and fall in love with a wood butcher
with a good heart and strong hands.
I don't know what my sisters were doing –
dipping bread into small dishes
of oil? – but I was already under
the sink, scrabbling for the organic
miracle cleaner. When I say organic
I mean no petroleum distillates,
no flammables, I mean . . . isn't there
a Chinese proverb, something
about stains and tablecloths, the more
stains the more delicious the meal?

I'm no good with details and my memory's
a garden of weeds, so I adjusted
the nozzle and aimed, and
never such an uproar, never so much
caterwauling over a drop of spilled
vegetable blood, all of us wailing,
Out, damned spot, out!

ORCHARD

The yellow plum in your hand
contains a childhood
that stretches so far back
it's the childhood of another girl,
girl you don't recognize who curls
her eyelashes at the bathroom
mirror, scrubs her face
with sand.

What does it mean to enter
the world lacking one of the senses?
What does it feel like to be a tree?

If you'd listened you might have heard
your mother calling but you had grown
lanky and abrasive, callous and needle-like.

When you see a tree
you think of its structure,
grace and age but do you think of
your mother? How, after death,
a veil lifted to reveal her inner rings?

And still you have no answers.
Does a tree speak in whispers?
Clap like thunder, crunch like gravel?

If you had ears you'd remember leaves
rustling outside your window. A corn
broom swishing down the path,
the wind coming up in late afternoon.
You'd remember moving your bedroom
furniture to rearrange the light.
But you were a child, deaf to the slurp
of water moving up a tree's trunk,
the *click click* of golden fruit being born.

RAISED ON RELIGION

Above the kitchen sink a wooden shoe
hung like a statue of Christ on the cross.

Sin and *retribution* my mother explained
three times a week as we passed through

heavy wooden doors. Outside in the parking
lot my father smoked *Players* in a truck

lacking a muffler. I shivered in the wilderness,
a parade of floats cruising past. Hard

candy, not manna, rained from heaven.
Not that it mattered, they were all going to die

a terrible death. That night I prayed for
my father and the go-go girls. I prayed for

the clowns. By then I was pilfering chalk
from the classroom. At home propped

my little sister in front of a blackboard
and taught her to read – *good bad, up down,*

black white. Early literacy, she'd tell me
years later, did her no good. Driving home

one night in winter – a three-car accident,
my father running through a downpour

to save a woman's life. And still the voice
from on high – and the unbelieving . . .

shall have their part in the burning lake.
Fire and brimstone, the second death.

THE EVOLUTIONARY BIOLOGIST
REMEMBERS THE HIGHLAND FLING

My Nana was robust though deaf in one ear
except when God was talking. He talked
non-stop in those days, voice travelling
down through the clouds and into
the kitchen where Nana spun
from kettle to frying pan. Me,
I wasn't good with liquids,
spilled the mixed nuts, broke
bones and china saucers, nor was I
adept at drinking through straws.
I squawked when the garbage
truck wheezed past her house, howled
when she turned on the vacuum.
Wheesht, hen, she'd say, paradise
is just around the bend. And death
would be no more. Death? My head
went through a glass window. Snapped back
so fast I came up unscathed. How could she know
that one day I'd crawl back to the origins
of things, discover the fossil of a creature
that lived eons before her god arrived
on the scene to scoop up handfuls of clay,
make heaven and earth in seven quick days?
Back then, I wanted to grow fins.
Anything that moved underwater
meant the world to me, a clumsy girl
whose brain kept changing.
And when a tartan cape appeared
on my pillow, I swooned joy.
If your mammy sees you, Nana laughed,
it'll be the death of me. Death? Again?

And I laughed too. Nana would never die,
Nana was forever. *Scotland the Brave*, she sang,
as I hopped up and down in front of the fireplace,
feet flicking just as she'd taught me,
hands above my head, heel-toe, heel-toe,
some sort of war dance, some sweet victory.

FIRST MOVIE

In a company town somewhere in northern Canada
a girl, six, maybe seven, holds onto her arm rests
as though about to launch into orbit. Her first movie,
The Adventures of Huckleberry Finn, 1961. Light dims
to darkness and then silence so utter she can hear
her own heartbeat. A beam explodes above her head
and the film's rolling, a rhythmic *tick, tick, tick.*

She leans forward, trying to understand
but confusion piles upon confusion, a man
beating a boy, slaughtered pig, riverboat, rainstorm,
raft bucking in waves. And then the runaway
slave is running away. The soundtrack detonates
gunfire and dogs barking. Men's boots crash
through underbrush. The runaway's face fills

the screen. His eyes. The enormous whites of his eyes.
Beads of sweat on his brow, a gash across his cheek.
He scrambles over fallen logs, splashes across creek beds.
Music, a rising crescendo that starts the girl whimpering.
Her older sister jabs her arm, but the girl whimpers louder.
The movie rolls on for hours, days, years, and the girl
grows up and gets married, has children of her own

to whom she tells stories, their favourite, the one about
the girl in a company town somewhere in northern Canada,
six, maybe seven, outside a theatre, bawling as her father's
Pontiac pulls up to the curb. From the backseat she hears
her sister say, *I'm not taking that crybaby anywhere again,*
but the girl doesn't care because her father is driving
away from the mighty Mississippi, he is driving far, far away.

GOOD LUCK STRANGER

Oh my papa, to me he was so wonderful.
Oh my papa, to me he was so good.
– Paul Burkhard, Geoffrey Parsons and John Turner

My grandfather worked in a sugar
factory bombed in the blitz. He was tall,
with dark hair, a teetotaler in a country of binge
drinkers.
          That's it.
That's all I know about the man
except neighbours would invite him into their houses
on January 1st, their good luck stranger.

I was five when I found my mother
sitting on the toilet seat, a flimsy blue aerogram
in her hand. Her father had died peacefully in his sleep,
she said, but today, hearing of a friend's death,
I'm not so sure. Today, for the first time,
I'm uncertain about my grandfather's death.

Fifty German bombers pummeled Greenock
in the spring of 1941. The start of a new moon.
Wild roses blooming along the hedgerows.
If he'd been working the night-shift,
my grandfather would not have lived.

What we know and what we think we know.
What we think we know but cannot possibly.

                    I know
I stood in a bathroom doorway,
looking at a woman I did not recognize.

I know she was weeping.
I think she was singing *Oh my papa* . . .

HEART WARD

My mother was the Scottish coastline and I'm
that way too, cold and ragged, the North Sea
pounding. She was also a significant river
port, a small book of Rabbie Burns poems,
a paper cup of mushy peas soaked in vinegar. Look
out the window and you'll see a black swan
spreading its wings on a church wall, dirty-kneed
children climbing an oak tree, heads lit against the sky.

My mother was all these things the night
she walked the halls of the Coronary Heart Ward
with my daughter, passing out Quality Street
chocolates and telling jokes. I am told
she was light on her feet, despite the walker,
radiant as a girl, stepping through buoyant spring air.
I am told she talked openly to strangers and fellow
patients, dragging IV poles. That even the harassed
nurses looked up and smiled as she passed their stations.

(I wasn't there the night my mother
was never more alive than when
she was hours away from death.)

I am not my mother, a woman who lived
most of her life in a foreign country, passport
close to her breast. I am not my daughter
who saw sixty-five starlings crash-land on the street
in front of her apartment on the last night
of my mother's life or the social worker,
who, the next morning, told me
it's not uncommon for the thing we call
the human spirit to flare up,
bright and incandescent,
moments before it gutters out.

TOWARD A LIST OF DEFINITIONS ACCORDING TO MY MOTHER

for Catherine

1. Blether (noun): person of either gender who talks incessantly about trivial matters.

2. Wee blether (adj./noun): child who talks incessantly about trivial matters, though not necessarily a child; a wee blether need only be a person of small stature.

3. Bletherer (noun): inter-changeable with blether.

4. Blethery (adj.): describes a person, usually a woman named Agnes or Maggie, who talks incessantly about trivial matters, though may also be a man named Jock or Billy, notably in his cups.

5. In his cups (colloquial): state of having consumed large quantities of whiskey.

6. For the love of the wee man, haud yer wheesht! (command; exasperated): given to, usually male, though not necessarily male, blether who has stumbled into the house in the wee hours in his cups, reeking like a distillery.

7. Distillery: (a) place of employment (b) source of rack and ruin.

8. Bism (noun): errant female child.

9. Cheeky bism (adj./noun): errant female child who, having been reprimanded, attempts to defend herself.

10. Cheek back (verb): defensive strategy of a bism who has been reprimanded for errant behaviour.

11. I'll smack ye, so I will (menacing but idle threat): uttered by (a) mother to child (b) blether to bism (c) bism to blether (d) Billy to Agnes (e) Maggie to Jock.

12. Wee hen (adj./noun): term of affection for female child who has apologized for (a) errant behaviour, and/or (b) cheeking back.

13. Gonnae no dae that nae mare: promise (usually broken) made by a man, woman or child to no longer (a) talk incessantly about trivial matters (b) consume great amounts of whiskey (c) utter menacing but idle threats (d) misbehave and/or attempt to defend oneself (so help me God).

LIFE SO FAR

Ate ephemera for breakfast,
all I could stomach.
Stashed the rest in the fridge
behind the ketchup.
Grew up like a magpie.
Scrawled *Magnum* and *Opus*
on the granite cenotaph
across from the church.
Spent the last year of high
school reading novels in bed.
Then ryegrass and broom.
Sneezing through spring.
Caught a train in Rotterdam.
Tulip fields blurred into
cathedrals into black
market yard sales.
Married. Gave birth. Beat
my father at ping-pong.
Smelled sage and creosote.
Watched a boy and girl walk
side by side into the desert.

BLUE MONDAY: WALKING THE WATERFRONT

The third Monday in January . . . is the most depressing
day of the year. – The Guardian

I was thinking about my friend who loved the world
but not too much to leave it; who in the end
decided music and art could not sustain the body

or bury the dead. I was thinking about the dead,
the unburied corpses piling up in Port-au-Prince,
how each day there were a few more minutes

of light. I was thinking about light, the surprise of it.
Each year the same surprise. On Blue Monday
snowdrops dropped their snowy heads, dogs lunged

after each other in the leash-less field, and I was
thinking about tears, more specifically, moths
that feed on the tears of sleeping birds, how those

moths will insert a harpoon-shaped proboscis
under a bird's eyelid, and drink. I was thinking how
all life forms devise and devour whatever they must

to survive. I passed a barefoot slack-rope walker
balancing on a slack rope strung between two trees
and thought about my friend who died in the house

she'd lived in for more than forty years, house her body
knew as home, and I thought, some deaths, surely,
are better than others. And the roller-bladers and old

ones in wheelchairs, the babies snug at their fathers'
breasts. I passed them all. Turning toward the breakwater,
I decided to be sad no longer. Besides, what can you

say to someone who's packed her bag, put on her coat?
Sometimes leaving is doing what you want, sometimes
what you want is to head out the door. She left.

Good for her. On Blue Monday I walked toward
the lighthouse beneath a gunmetal sky, eying the cruise
ship parked in the strait, dumb as a thought, and then

for no reason I remembered my daughter at three,
saying, *I hate the stars, the stars are scary. Then look at
the moon*, I said. *Oh, the moon*, she said, *I love the moon!*

THE NEW BABY: A SERIES OF GIGANS

1. PREGNANT WOMAN

She made a single cupcake with a candle on top,
in a house not her own, that she couldn't seem to leave

because pieces of herself had gone missing.
She wandered in and out of rooms, down hallways,
searching for fingers and anklebones, freckles and earlobes.

How dilapidated, how upside down.
Cracked windows, collapsed banisters, rotting plaster.

She tripped over buckled floorboards, reached for light
switches that weren't there. *This way*, a voice said,

so she followed up a narrow staircase, into an attic room
where she made a single cupcake with a candle on top.

How dilapidated, how upside down.
A zigzag of hand-dyed skeins pegged out
with rows of ragged clothing. It seemed a long line of
            mothers

had been there before her. All night they'd been washing
bonnets and nightgowns and little woolen coats.

2. GRANDPARENTS

The month before the baby was born they scrabbled in the dirt.
Dug the last root vegetables out of the ground.

Dragged the gate-leg table into the living room and ate
roasted parsnips in front of the fire. They rarely spoke
and when they did it was to wonder about the baby.

Was she a he? Was he a she?
Day after day, night after night: their concentrated waiting.

And then the phone call, pre-dawn news breaking
like water: their daughter had gone into labour.

In silence they drove up the ramp into the ferry's hollow belly.
The month before they'd scrabbled in dirt. The unborn baby –

was she a he? Was he a she?
In the Sea West Lounge they sat across from each other,
green islands submerged in low cloud.

They hardly spoke and when they did it was to wonder about
            the baby –
had she kicked off yet? Had he arrived like a small tug?

3. NEWBORN

How like a fat slug.
Or blind mole, burrowing.

An ancient from some other place where speech
is amber and you can't help wondering
where the light's coming from.

When laid on his stomach how like a frog,
hairless and absurd.

How spacey and unformed,
serious and equipped –

the suck and grasp, the gut-searing cry.
How like a fat slug.

When laid on his stomach how like a frog,
remote and alien,
milk-duct sensitive.

How small the toenails.
How big the brain.

4. PRE-VERBAL

Shilly-shallying, the parents called it.
Look, he's shilly-shallying again.

Legs kicking, fists clenched in front of his body:
small engine in overdrive. But when they bent over him,
melon heads blocking the sun,

he relaxed and turned his head away.
Stared at the torch lilies and began to speak,

inchoate sound rolling off his tongue
in a measured soliloquy. That day in the back garden

they understood the words of every language
were contained within the jewel box of his throat.
Shilly-shallying, they called it

when he stared at the torch lilies and began to speak,
and it was like watching phonemes
catch fire

and spread across the globe
like the first human migration.

5. LULLABY

He arched his back. Busted out of his swaddle.
Refused one breast so I offered the other.

I re-swaddled him. He busted out again.
I walked the apartment, baby flailing against my chest.
Sat on the toilet seat and turned on the bath tap.

I let the water run full force because I hoped
the sound of running water would calm the baby.

Water splashed against the tiles, bubbled
down the drain, surged through wall pipes,

out to the street and into the ocean.
He arched his back. Busted out of his swaddle.

I let the water run full force because
I was drowning in cymbals and sirens. White noise
coursed through phone lines and radio waves,

bandwidths and electrical wires.
Water, I sang to the baby, *water, water*.

6. NIGHTMARE

When I arrive at the box store it's midnight and shoppers
in party hats are pushing carts up and down aisles.

Blue lights flash: *Special! Special!*
Was I careless with the baby? Had he rolled off
the table when I turned to wave at the tourists

passing the window in horse-drawn carriages?
Had he slipped between the couch cushions

when I went into the change room to try on skinny jeans?
One minute I'm holding the baby, laughing at his goofy
       expressions,

and the next he's an ice-cube melting in my drink.
When I arrive at the box store it's midnight and shoppers

are passing the window in horse-drawn carriages.
Every shabby item's marked down to nothing.
I drop to my knees, run my fingers

through the shag carpet, searching for a button,
lipstick sample, thumbtack in the light-saturated grass.

7. EXHAUSTION

After a night of no sleep the new mother
pushes the stroller through the cemetery's tree-lined paths.

Every morning she finds herself here, in a daze,
gulping coffee from an aluminum travel mug, thinking,
This is where we all end up, in soft beds, thank god, never
        to be woken.

The smell of cut grass, mounds of fresh dirt.
A tractor mower droning the distance. And beyond –

traffic, the shush of waves. Pregnant, she imagined it all
differently. Saw herself jogging the waterfront, pushing
        the baby

in his high-tech chariot with its seven shock absorbers.
Another night of no sleep. The new mother

inhaling cut grass, mounds of fresh dirt,
one leaden foot falling in front of the other.
Mausoleums crumble around her, gravestones sink deeper,

and the baby in his fleece bunting suit
babbles ecstatic.

Acknowledgements

I would like to thank the editors of the following magazines in which some of these poems first appeared: *The Antigonish Review* – "The Evolutionary Biologist Remembers the Highland Fling," "The Shortest Distance," "The Roofers"; *Canadian Literature* – "Mermaid," "Wall of Fire"; CV2 – "Heart Ward"; *The Dalhousie Review* – "First Date"; *The Literary Review of Canada* – "Footnote to Genesis"; *The Malahat Review* – "Daughter at Thirteen"; *The New Quarterly* – "Blue Monday," "The New Baby – A Series of Gigans"; *Prism International* – "The Big Siesta (or the End of Modern Warfare)," "Toward a List of Definitions According to My Scottish Mother"; *Room* – "Morning Class"; *Queen's Quarterly* – "Sixties Secretaries"; *Stinging Fly* – "Family Real Estate."

"Morning Class" won the *Room* poetry contest.

"Blue Monday" placed second in *New Quarterly*'s Occasional Verse contest.

"The Roofers," "The Evolutionary Biologist Remembers the Highland Fling," and "The Shortest Distance" placed third in the *Antigonish Review*'s Great Blue Heron Contest.

"Daughter at Thirteen" was shortlisted in the *Malahat Review*'s Open Season Award.

"The Big Siesta (or the End of Modern Warfare)" and "Toward a List of Definitions According to my Scottish Mother" were honourable mentions in *Prism International*'s poetry contest in different years.

"The Big Siesta" was included in *The Best Canadian Poetry in English*, 2011, edited by Priscila Uppal (Tightrope Books).

"This Evening the Swabbies" was published in *The Montreal International Poetry Prize Anthology* e-book, and "Tamarind Tree" was published in *The Montreal International Poetry Prize Global Anthology* (Vehicule Press, 2012).

I would like to thank the B.C. Arts Council for financial assistance received during the writing of this manuscript.

Also many thanks to the marvelous and enduring lfc and fb's. As always, my deepest thanks to Terence, first and best reader.

OTHER QUATTRO POETRY BOOKS